THE PLANETARY SOCIETY

T0112989

MERCURY

A WORLD OF EXTREMES

Bruce Betts, PhD

Lerner Publications ◆ Minneapolis

THE PLANETS AND MOONS IN OUR SOLAR SYSTEM ARE OUT OF THIS WORLD. Some are hotter than an oven, and some are much colder than a freezer. Some are small and rocky, while others are huge and mostly made of gas. As you explore these worlds, you'll discover giant canyons, active volcanoes, strange kinds of ice, storms bigger than Earth, and much more.

The Planetary Society® empowers people around the world to advance space science and exploration. On behalf of The Planetary Society®, including our tens of thousands of members, here's wishing you the joy of discovery.

Onward,

Bill Nye

Bill Nye
CEO, The Planetary Society®

TABLE OF CONTENTS

CHAPTER 1

A WORLD OF EXTREMES

Our solar system is huge! It includes everything that goes around the Sun. The Sun is the center of our solar system.

There are eight planets. They all circle the Sun. We live on Earth. Earth is the third planet from the Sun.

Mercury is the closest planet to the Sun. It is about 36 million miles (58 million km) from the Sun. That is less than half the distance between the Sun and Earth.

A photo of Mercury taken by a spacecraft

What if you could stand on the surface of Mercury and look at the Sun? The Sun would appear three times bigger than it does from Earth!

MERCURY FAST FACTS

Size	Could fit about eighteen Mercurys inside Earth
Distance from the Sun	About 36 million miles (58 million km)
Length of day	176 Earth days
Length of year	88 Earth days
Number of moons	0

MEET MERCURY

Mercury can get very hot and very cold. Mercury gets a lot hotter than Earth because it is much closer to the Sun. It can reach 800°F (430°C) during the day. That is hotter than an oven!

But Mercury also gets very cold at night. That is because it

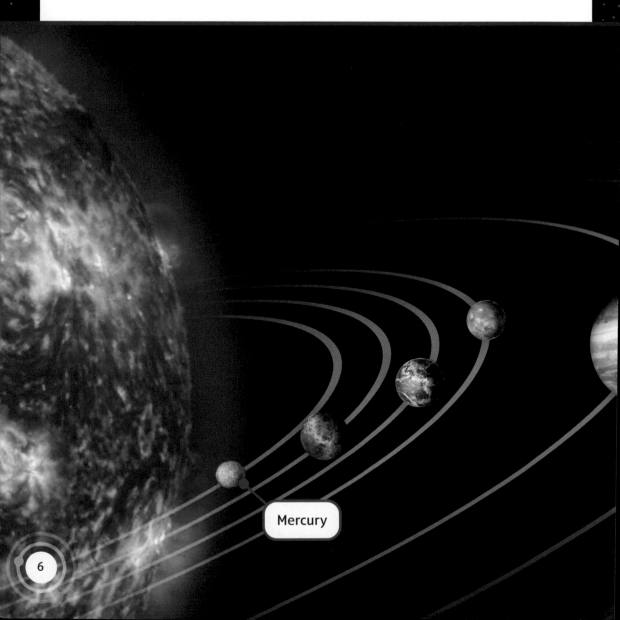

Mercury

doesn't have an atmosphere. An atmosphere is made of the gases that cover some planets. These gases hold heat like a blanket.

Mercury gets as low as −290°F (−180°C) at night. That is much colder than a freezer! Nighttime on Mercury lasts almost three Earth months.

The closer a planet circles the Sun, the faster it goes. Mercury travels faster than any of our other planets because it is closest to the Sun.

Speedy

Planet Mercury is named after the Roman god Mercury because of its speed. Mercury was the speedy messenger of the Roman gods.

A statue of the Roman god Mercury

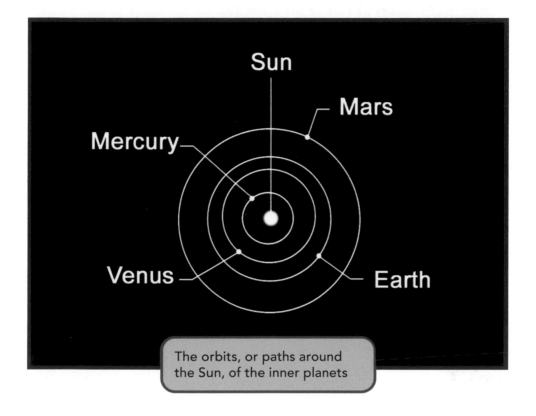

The orbits, or paths around the Sun, of the inner planets

A day is the time a planet takes to spin around from noon to noon. One day on Earth is twenty-four hours. Mercury spins much slower than Earth. One day on Mercury is about 176 Earth days.

A year is the time it takes a planet to go all the way around the Sun. One Earth year is about 365 days. One Mercury year is only about 88 Earth days. That means one day on Mercury is longer than one year on Mercury!

MERCURY AND OTHER PLANETS

The four planets closest to the Sun are Mercury, Venus, Earth, and Mars. They are called the inner planets. They are also called the rocky planets because they have rocky surfaces. These planets are mostly made of rocks and metals.

The four planets farthest from the Sun are Jupiter, Saturn, Uranus, and Neptune. They are called the outer planets. They are also called giant planets because they are very large.

Left to right: Mercury, Venus, Earth, and Mars are the four rocky planets.

The Smallest Planet

Mercury is our smallest planet. It's much smaller than Earth but bigger than Earth's Moon. If Mercury were the size of a softball, Earth would be the size of a basketball.

The center of a planet is called the core. Earth's and Mercury's cores are made of metal. Mercury's core is different from that of other planets because it is very big for the size of the planet.

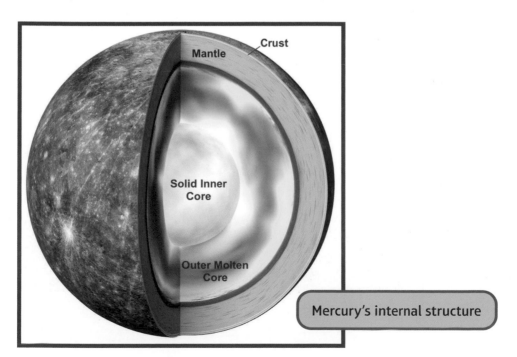

Crust
Mantle
Solid Inner Core
Outer Molten Core

Mercury's internal structure

CHAPTER 2

PLANET OF CRATERS

You can sometimes see Mercury in the night sky with just your eyes. Mercury looks like a bright star. We can see the planet even better by using special tools such as telescopes.

CRATERS

Mercury looks a lot like Earth's Moon. They are both gray and covered in holes shaped like bowls. These holes are called craters. Craters are made when space rocks hit the ground really fast.

The surface of Mercury (*left*) compared to Earth's Moon (*right*)

Craters on Mercury are named after famous artists, musicians, and authors. One is named after the author Dr. Seuss.

One group of craters looks like a Mickey Mouse head. The largest of these craters is named Disney after Walt Disney. Walt Disney created Mickey Mouse.

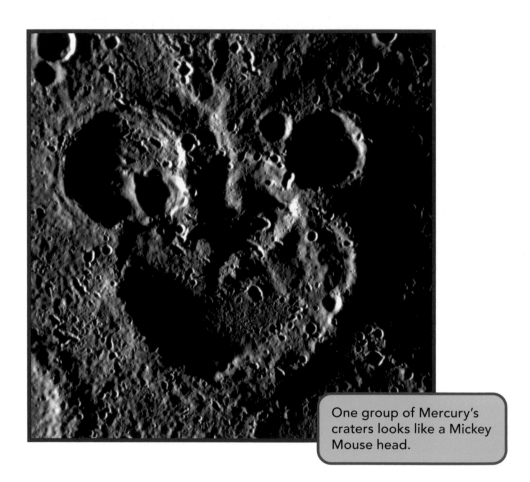

One group of Mercury's craters looks like a Mickey Mouse head.

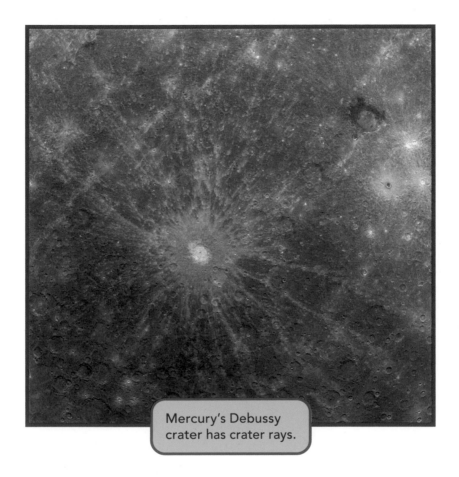

Mercury's Debussy crater has crater rays.

Some craters have long bright lines that go out in every direction. These lines are called crater rays. They are made when space rocks hit the ground and make rocks and dirt fly very far in all directions.

MOUNTAINS

Mercury has long mountain ranges called wrinkle ridges. These ridges were made as Mercury shrank over billions of years.

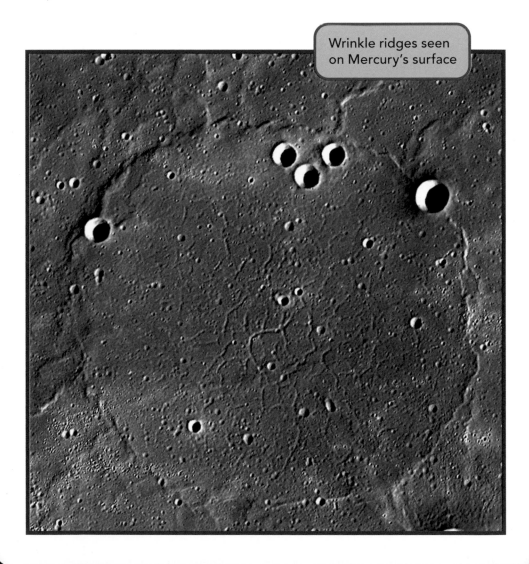

Wrinkle ridges seen on Mercury's surface

No Air

Earth has air for us to breathe. But Mercury does not have air. You would need to wear a space suit on Mercury since there is nothing to breathe.

CHAPTER 3

EXPLORING MERCURY

Astronauts have only visited Earth's Moon. The planets are too far away from Earth for humans to travel to. We can learn some things about the planets and our solar system from Earth. But we use spacecraft to learn much more.

Spacecraft can study the planets up close and help us to better understand them. Scientists have explored Mercury with three spacecraft. They are Mariner 10, MESSENGER, and BepiColombo.

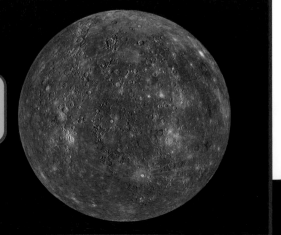

This collection of many images of one side of Mercury uses data from MESSENGER.

SPACECRAFT

Mariner 10 was the first to explore Mercury. It left Earth in 1973. Mariner 10 had its first flyby of Mercury in 1974. It did a total of three flybys.

Mariner 10 gave us our first look at Mercury's surface. But it only saw one side of the planet.

Mariner 10 also found that Mercury has a magnetic field. That is the area around a magnet where there is a magnetic force.

This is a collection of many images of Mercury taken by Mariner 10.

MESSENGER left Earth in 2004. It had its first of three flybys of Mercury in 2008. It saw the side of Mercury that Mariner 10 missed.

In 2011, MESSENGER became the first spacecraft to circle Mercury. It spent the next few years getting new information about the planet. It also took better photos of Mercury.

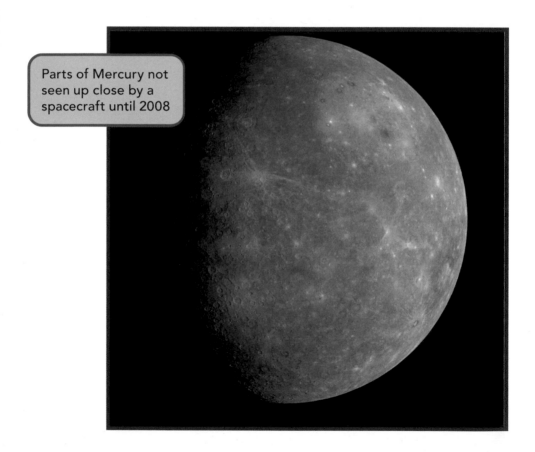

Parts of Mercury not seen up close by a spacecraft until 2008

Staying Cool

The Sun can harm some parts of spacecraft. Since Mercury is the closest planet to the Sun, spacecraft need special protection from the Sun to explore Mercury. MESSENGER had a sun shield for protection.

MESSENGER's special protective sun shield

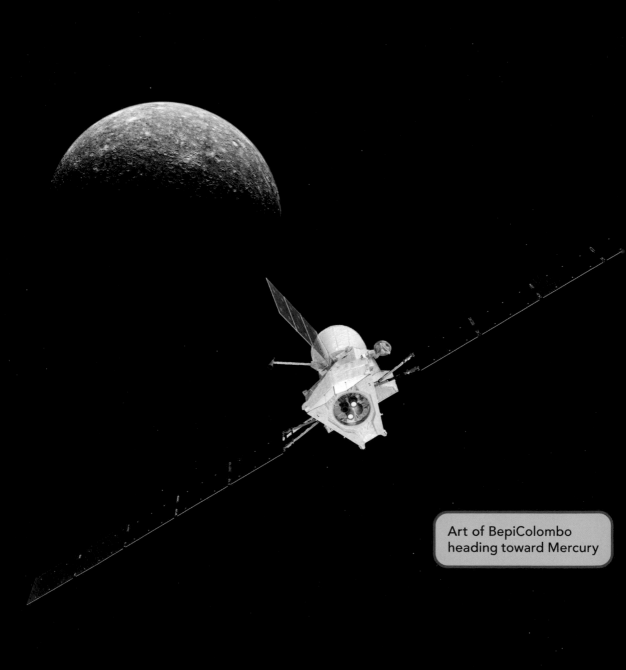

Art of BepiColombo
heading toward Mercury

BepiColombo left Earth in 2018. It had its first flyby of Mercury in 2021, and more were planned.

BepiColombo is made up of two spacecraft. They were planned to separate in 2025 and begin to circle Mercury.

One of the spacecraft is for studying Mercury's surface. The other is for studying Mercury's magnetic field.

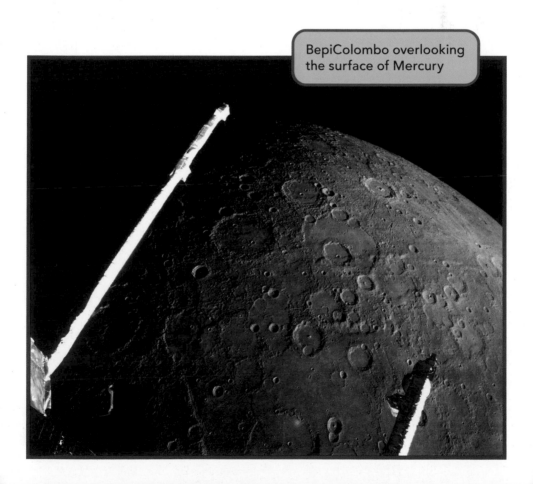

BepiColombo overlooking the surface of Mercury

Mercury in Color

Mercury would look gray if you were on its surface. But our eyes can't see as much as spacecraft can. They have tools that see types of light we can't see.

This is a color image of one side of Mercury.

Scientists use these tools to learn what a planet's surface is made of. Then they make a color photo of Mercury based on what they have learned. Scientists use colors we can see in place of colors we can't see.

One of Mercury's huge craters looks like an orange circle in this photo. The areas around the crater are different colors. They are made of different kinds of rocks than the crater.

A color photo of Mercury's Caloris Basin crater

NEW FINDINGS

Mercury has water ice in the bottom of craters near its north and south poles. The bottoms of those craters stay cold because they never see sunlight.

These yellow spots show locations of water ice in Mercury's north pole.

Mercury has hollows. Hollows are holes inside craters. They often look bright in pictures. Scientists haven't found them anywhere else in the solar system.

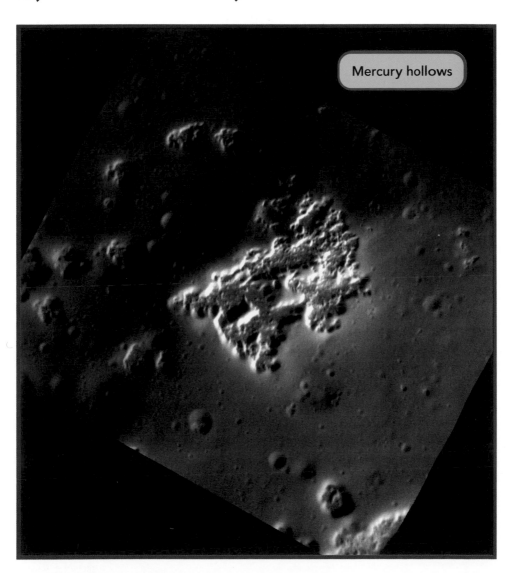

Mercury hollows

Mercury is an amazing planet. We will learn more about this small, speedy planet as we keep exploring our solar system. And it is only one of our eight planets. Have fun and keep learning more!

We will keep learning more about Mercury's surface.

BepiColombo
leaving Earth in 2018

Glossary

atmosphere: the gases surrounding a planet, moon, or other body

core: the center of a planet or moon

crater: a bowl-shaped hole caused by space rocks hitting the ground at high speeds

day: the time it takes a planet to spin around from noon to noon. One Earth day is about twenty-four hours long.

flyby: a spacecraft's flight passing by a planet for observation

magnetic field: the area around a magnet where there is a magnetic force

planet: a big, round, ball-shaped object that only goes around the Sun. Our solar system has eight planets. A planet does not have anything close to the same size near its orbit.

spacecraft: a vehicle or object made for travel in outer space

year: the time it takes a planet to go all the way around the Sun. One Earth year is about 365 days long.

Learn More

Bassier, Emma. *Mercury*. Minneapolis: Cody Koala, 2021.

Betts, Bruce, PhD. *Casting Shadows: Solar and Lunar Eclipses with The Planetary Society®*. Minneapolis: Lerner Publications, 2024.

Lawrence, Ellen. *Mercury: The High-Speed Planet*. Chicago: Sequoia Kids Media, 2022.

NASA Space Place: All about Mercury
https://spaceplace.nasa.gov/all-about-mercury/en/

National Geographic Kids: Mission to Mercury
https://kids.nationalgeographic.com/space/article/mission-to-mercury

The Planetary Society: Mercury, World of Extremes
https://www.planetary.org/worlds/mercury

INDEX

PHOTO ACKNOWLEDGMENTS

Image credits: The Planetary Society, p. 2; NASA/JHUAPL/CIW/color mosaic by Jason Perry/The Planetary Society, p. 4; NASA/JPL, pp. 6, 7, 19; Bruce Yuanyue Bi/Getty Images, p. 8; Betts/The Planetary Society, p. 9; NASA/Wikimedia Commons (PD), p. 10; NASA's Goddard Space Flight Center, p. 11; miljko/Getty Images, p. 12; NASA/JPL/Space Science Institute, p. 13; NASA/Johns Hopkins University Applied Physics Laboratory/Carnegie Institution of Washington, pp. 13, 14, 15, 16, 18, 20, 21, 24, 27, 28; Universal Images Group North America LLC/Alamy, p. 17; ESA/ATG medialab and NASA/JPL, p. 22; ESA/BepiColombo/MTM, p. 23; Image produced by NASA/Johns Hopkins University Applied Physics Laboratory/Arizona State University/Carnegie Institution of Washington. Image reproduced courtesy of Science/AAAS., p. 25; NASA/Johns Hopkins University Applied Physics Laboratory/Carnegie Institution of Washington/National Astronomy and Ionosphere Center, Arecibo Observatory, p. 26; JODY AMIET/AFP/Getty Images, p. 29. Design elements: Sergey Balakhnichev/Getty Images; Baac3nes/Getty Images; Elena Kryulena/Shutterstock; Anna Frajtova/Shutterstock.
Cover: NASA/NASA/Johns Hopkins University Applied Physics Laboratory/Carnegie Institution of Washington.

FOR MY SONS, KEVIN AND DANIEL, AND FOR ALL THE MEMBERS OF THE PLANETARY SOCIETY®

Lerner Publications Company
An imprint of Lerner Publishing Group, Inc.
241 First Avenue North
Minneapolis, MN 55401 USA

For reading levels and more information, look up this title at www.lernerbooks.com.

Main body text set in Aptifer Sans LT Pro. Typeface provided by Linotype AG.

Editor: Brianna Kaiser **Designer:** Mary Ross
Lerner team: Sue Marquis

Library of Congress Cataloging-in-Publication Data

Names: Betts, Bruce (PhD), author.
Title: Mercury : a world of extremes / Bruce Betts, PhD.
Description: Minneapolis, MN : Lerner Publications, [2025] | Series: Exploring our solar system with the Planetary Society | Includes bibliographical references and index. | Audience: Ages 7–10 | Audience: Grades 2–3 | Summary: "The smallest planet in our solar system, Mercury is a world of extremes. And it's the closest planet to our Sun! Explore fun facts about Mercury, the planet's surface, and more"— Provided by publisher.
Identifiers: LCCN 2023033615 (print) | LCCN 2023033616 (ebook) | ISBN 9798765626818 (library binding) | ISBN 9798765628645 (paperback) | ISBN 9798765633281 (epub)
Subjects: LCSH: Mercury (Planet)—Juvenile literature.
Classification: LCC QB611 .B48 2025 (print) | LCC QB611 (ebook) | DDC 523.41—dc23/eng/20231018

LC record available at https://lccn.loc.gov/2023033615
LC ebook record available at https://lccn.loc.gov/2023033616

Manufactured in the United States of America
1-1009900-52012-10/25/2023